hazelnuts
from
Julian of Norwich

Meditations on Divine Love

Copyright © 2018 by Anamchara Books, a division of Harding House Publishing Service, Inc. Aside from short quotations, appropriately credited, this book may not be reproduced or transmitted in any form or by any means, electronic or mechanical, including photocopying, recording, taping, or any information storage and retrieval system, without permission from the publisher.

Printed in the United States of America.

9 8 7 6 5 4 3 2 1

ANAMCHARA BOOKS
Vestal, NY 13850
www.AnamcharaBooks.com

Design by Micaela Grace.

IngramSpark 2020 paperback ISBN:
978-1-62524-803-9

HAZELNUTS
FROM
JULIAN OF NORWICH

MEDITATIONS ON DIVINE LOVE

Ellyn Sanna, Editor

ANAMCHARA
BOOKS

CONTENTS

Introduction	7
I. The Divine One	21
II. The Soul	67
III. Sin and Sorrow	117
IV. The Meaning of Julian's Vision	161

INTRODUCTION

The Spirit showed me a tiny thing the size of a hazelnut, as round as a ball and so small I could hold it in the palm of my hand. I looked at it in my mind's eye and wondered, "What is this?" The answer came to me: "This is everything that has been made. This is all Creation." It was so small that I marveled it could endure; such a tiny thing seemed likely to simply fall into nothingness. Again the answer came to my thoughts: "It lasts, and it will always last, because God loves it." Everything—all that exists—draws its being from God's love.

The woman who wrote these words, known today as Julian of Norwich, was born in late 1342, and she died around 1412. We do not know her given name or much else about her. ("Saint Julian's" was the name of the church to which she attached herself.) Some scholars suggest that Julian may have outlived a husband and children, and as I have gotten to know her through spending so many years studying her words, I have come to believe that the images she used in her writing indicate she understood motherhood firsthand. Other scholars disagree, however, and suggest that instead, she was a nun who entered a convent at a very early age. Either way, we can only speculate, for we have few confirmed historical details of her life.

We do know that by the time she was a young woman, she had seen many in her community succumb to the Black Death. During her lifetime, the Plague swept through England three times, and Norwich was particularly hard hit; at least half the population died from the Plague. Death was so commonplace that the clergy and undertakers could not keep up with the corpses. Grace Jantzen, author of *Julian of Norwich: Mystic and Theologian* (Paulist Press) vividly describes the reality that Julian and the others in her community would have experienced:

> People died, horribly and suddenly and in great numbers. It was so contagious that one contemporary witness describes how anyone who touched the sick or the dead immediately caught the disease and died himself [sic], so that priests who ministered to the dying were flung into the same grave with their penitents. It was impossible for the clergy to keep up with all those who required last rites, and to die unshriven was seen as a catastrophe of eternal proportions. Nor could the people who died be buried with dignity. . . . The psychological impact on the survivors was incalculable, made worse in subsequent years by the further outbreaks which occurred at unpredictable intervals.

Julian's era was one of terrible turmoil and crisis. While people were dying of the Plague, other diseases killed the cattle, and harvests failed, causing famines and more death and disease. In 1381, people became so desperate they rose up in a revolt, looting the churches and monasteries. Meanwhile, John Wyclif was preaching against the corruption within the Church; his translation of the Bible into the common language of English brought down on him papal accusations of heresy, and his followers were burned alive in a pit less than a mile from Julian's cell. (She would have breathed the ashes of their bodies, carried to her on the wind.) The larger world beyond Norwich and England was also in a state of upheaval. Five years before Julian was born, in 1337, the Hundred Years War between England and France had begun, and it would continue throughout her lifetime. The Great Schism split the Church in 1377, with one pope in France, the other in Rome. And in the midst of all this, Julian came to believe unshakably that "all shall be well, and all shall be well, and all manner of things shall be well."

She was not immune, however, to the very real pain of human life. In fact, I suspect that survivor guilt may have been what drove her to plead with God to send her suffering and sickness. She must have asked herself why she was spared when so many around her died. In any event, in May 1373, when Julian was thirty-one, her prayers were granted and she became so sick that a priest was called to administer the last rites.

This experience became the turning point of her life. While she lay on what she thought was her deathbed, she had intense mystical revelations, which she called "showings"—a series of visual, auditory, and emotional experiences, probably the result of a fevered brain, from which she garnered incredible insights into Divine Love. She did not die, but recovered from her illness—and for the next twenty years, she pondered her visions, using them to shape a joyful affirmation of God's true nature.

At some point in her life, she became an anchoress, committed to a life of prayer and meditation while confined to a cell adjoining a church. Anchoresses—women who chose to be imprisoned for God—were an accepted part of medieval life. Although they had opted for a living burial, dying to the world in a very practical way, these women continued to be active in their communities, serving a function rather like a counselor or psychologist might today. Nobility and commoners, rich and poor, would have come to Julian's window, seeking her advice and guidance.

An anchoress's life was governed by a "rule," a written structure that prevented excess and abuse. Julian would have probably followed the Ancrene Rule, written early in the thirteenth century, which provided detailed instructions for an anchoress's life. As a result, she would have worn plain clothes and eaten simple meals while living in a small suite of rooms. Her anchorage would have had three windows: one that looked into the church, through which she could listen to mass and receive communion; a second that opened into the outside world, allowing people to speak with her and hear her counsel; and a third that looked into an adjoining room, where a servant lived. Unlike Julian, the servant could come and go, entering Julian's suite to bring food and do the cooking and cleaning, so that Julian's time could be devoted completely to prayer and spiritual counsel. She would have also been allowed a cat, for companionship and to battle rodents.

Julian's life as an anchoress gave her plenty of time to ponder the revelations she had received. She wrote first a short text, describing what she had seen on her sickbed, and then, as she further analyzed and meditated on her "showings," she wrote a longer text that vividly described all God had revealed to her.

Her book was the first to be written by a woman in the English language. At about the same time, Geoffrey Chaucer was also writing in the English of the era, but Chaucer had a sophisticated educational heritage

Julian lacked. Her English was the ordinary vocabulary of common people. Some scholars believe she was unable to even read and write at the time of her revelation, and that she taught herself what she needed to know in order to record and pass on what God had shown her. Educated or not, her mind was brilliant and sharp, able to grasp subtle meaning in even the simplest experiences and to combine that with a deep theological comprehension.

After her death, Julian's writing survived in copies made by nuns and guarded in convents. Because of the risk of being accused of heresy (an accusation that could be fatal in the Middle Ages), the book was not printed until 1670. Through the centuries, its wisdom was like a quiet, shining stream, influencing many spiritual seekers. Over the past century, it has regained a new popularity, partly because of Julian's strong feminine images of God and Jesus. In recent years, a flood of new books based on Julian's work has been published, as well as new translations, including my *All Shall Be*

Well: A Modern-Language Version of the Revelation of Julian of Norwich, which forms the basis of the poem-prayers included in the book that follows here.

Much of the religious language that has become the jargon of modern Christianity had its origins in the medieval period. Figures of speech that grew from the ordinary life of the Middle Ages (or the still more ancient Bible times) no longer have the same strength and liveliness today that they did when they were rooted in everyday experience. When we use these phrases, we think we know what we mean—but the meaning has faded and lost its energy. In some cases, a word's use has shifted so much that we lose sight of the spiritual truth that once underlay it.

The word "lord" is a good example of this. During the Middle Ages, the feudal hierarchy was the structure upon which society was built. It was necessary for the well-being and order of the community, as well as the safety of the individual. Today, we remember the hierarchy and often forget why it was necessary. To "lord it over someone" speaks of superiority versus inferiority, and we bring those connotations to any conversation with God in which we refer to the Divine as "Lord." But that meaning of the word did not show up in written English until the years just after Julian's death; in her day, the Old English word meant "keeper, guardian," and a lord's most vital function was to protect those under his care. Because of this, when I wrote my modern translation of Julian's book, *All Shall Be Well*, I replaced the word "Lord" with "Protector." This brings us closer to Julian's understanding of the word—and I hope the less familiar word will gives us a fresh awareness of our relationship with Christ.

Gender is also an issue I addressed in my translation of Julian's showings. Julian was perfectly comfortable speaking of Christ as a mother, using the masculine pronoun to describe feminine aspects of the Divine. Modern feminist theology often claims Julian as one of its earliest proponents, but the term "feminism" would have meant nothing to Julian. Instead, she was totally focused on the Divine reality revealed during her mystical experience, a reality expressed through gender even as it transcended gender. Here again, I endeavored to build into my translation of her book a similar transparency by using feminine pronouns where modern readers would be more comfortable using them, masculine pronouns where those make most sense—and using nongendered language where possible to be certain that the language I used to describe God is as inclusive as possible. Julian's English did not offer her this option, but ours does, and I believe that if Julian were writing today, she would gladly use inclusive language and extend some of her feminine metaphors for God to their more logical lengths.

Julian's message was written in ordinary language intended for ordinary people. She wrote at the end of her book, "This book is begun by God's gift, by Divine grace, but I do not believe it has yet been finished. It is still developing and growing." I wrote *All Shall Be*

Well in service to her lifelong labor, so that her book will continue to grow and develop in the twenty-first century, and the short, poem-prayer selections included here, arranged thematically, are intended to also further Julian's vision of Divine Love, given to us simply, sweetly, accessibly . . . promising us that in the midst of political turmoil, violence, disaster, accidents, and dread, we are always kept safe, enfolded in Love.

—Ellyn Sanna

1

THE
DIVINE
ONE

The Divine One says,

"I am.

I am the One:

I am the One who is highest,

I am the One you love,

I am all that you enjoy,

I am what you serve,

I am that which you long for most,

I am all that you desire,

I am who lives in your thoughts,

I am everything."

God is the ground

and the essence,

the teaching and the teacher,

the motive and the reward.

God is everything that is good,

everything that comforts,

everything that gives us pleasure.

The Spirit is our clothing, for in love,

the Divine One wraps us up,

holds us tight,

and encloses us with tenderness.

And since the Spirit lives everywhere,

in the entire universe,

how could we ever be abandoned?

Just as our bodies are clothed with fabrics;

our blood and muscles covered with skin;

our bones wrapped with blood and muscles;

and our hearts hidden at the center of all these,

so are we, soul and body,

clad in the goodness of God,

completely enclosed and safe.

~~~~~~

Our clothing, our flesh, our very bones,

may all grow old and waste away—

but the sweet unity of God

is always whole and strong.

Contained within redeemed humanity

is everything—all Creation and its Maker

—for God is in humanity,

and God is in all,

and so everything is united

into a single Body.

This is the Divine Body,

the Holy Flesh,

and when a human being loves

others in that Body,

she is loving all Creation.

I saw God contained in a tiny particle,
a Point so infinitesimal it could barely be seen
and yet it contained the origin
and essence of all things.
The Point was all reality,
and it contained no separation from God,
no separation from the love
that sustains the world.

~~~~~~

God is the Midpoint of all things,
the center on which the world turns.

The Divine Essence is in each thing that exists.

All actions are simply a going forth

of that Essence.

That is why there is no Doer but God.

God is the only Verb,

the single Action that moves

through every deed.

The Divine One says,

"I complete all things,

leading them to the goal

I set for them without any beginning,

by the same strength, wisdom, and love

through which I created them.

When this is the case,

how can anything

ultimately

be wrong with the world?"

The substance of all things

flows out from God

to work the Divine Will.

The same strength, wisdom,

and love that created the world

also continue to work within all Creation,

bringing each and every thing to God.

One day, we shall be able to see this is true.

The Divine Essence fits all things together

perfectly and sweetly.

It is the substance of reality,

the essence of all that is.

The Divine One
serves us in the simplest
and most ordinary ways.
Think how neatly our food
is contained within our bodies, digested,
and then emptied out as needed
through a lovely drawstring purse
that opens and closes.
None of our bodies' activities
offend the Divine Presence,
for even our natural functions
are vehicles of love.

The Divine Essence lives in many forms.

Nature—all that has been born into life—

is sweet and beautiful.

Nature went out from God,

and then Grace was sent out

to bring Nature back home

and destroy all that would undo it,

to bring Nature back to the holy Point

from which it first came,

even more high and worthy now,

because of Grace,

than it was in the beginning.

Nature and Grace are in agreement,

for Grace is God,

and Nature is God.

God works in these two ways,

but Divine love is united and singular.

Nature and Grace cannot be separated;

they work together.

God loved us before we were made,

and when we were made, we loved God.

This love is made from the Spirit's substance,

made active by the strength of God the Parent,

and made wise by the vision of God the Child.

At the same point where our souls spring to life,

created by God from God,

there we are sewn tight to God.

~~~~~~~~~~

Our most primal substance

springs from God.

Mercy and Grace

are two expressions of a single love.

Mercy—compassion—expresses Motherhood,

the Divine Feminine who is tender and loving,

while Grace is the Fatherhood,

that affirms our worth.

Mercy shelters us, brings us to life,

endures all pain, and heals us.

Grace lifts us up, gazes at us with pride,

and fulfills our hearts' desires.

This is the largeness, the bounty

of Divine love.

I saw completely and certainly

that before we were ever made,

we were loved.

~~~~~~~

Divine love for us has no beginning.

Just as we are intended for endless bliss,

fulfilling the everlasting joy

that flows through all Creation,

just so we were always known by God

and always loved,

without any beginning.

The intent of Christ, the Holy Go-Between,

was always aimed directly

toward the end-goal of love.

The Trinity was in accord with this intention;

the Divine "Yes" was spoken

from before the beginning of time.

Jesus the Go-Between
is the Founder of the human family,
the Source of our nature and life,
from whom we all spring,
the Womb that encloses us all.

~~~~~~~~~

We shall all wind our way back
into this Go-Between,
finding there our total Heaven,
our everlasting joy,
as was intended all along.

When Grace allows us to catch a glimpse

of God's sweetness,

we see no wrath there,

for wrath and friendship are opposite forces.

We are endlessly made one with God,

and no anger separates us.

~~~~~~~

How could the Divine One,

who is all gentleness and humility,

look at us with anger?

Our lives are grounded

and rooted in love;

without love,

we would not be alive.

~~~~~~~~

Everything—all that exists—

draws its being from God's love.

God's love for us has never diminished,

and it never will.

In this love, all Creation was made

and continues to live.

In this love, all things work out for our good;

and in this love,

we shall live forever.

The essence of our being

is complete

in each Person of the Trinity,

who is one God.

These three properties

are at work in the Trinity—

the Fatherhood,

the Motherhood,

and the Protection—

all One God.

The Trinity's high strength is our Father;

the Trinity's deep wisdom is our Mother;

and the Trinity's great love is our Protector.

These Three are ours,

woven into the nature and substance

of our being.

Our entire life is threefold:

in the first aspect, we have our being;

in the second, we have our growth;

and in the third, we have our fulfillment.

The first is our Nature,

the second Mercy,

and the third Grace.

Our High Father,
God All-Strong who is Being itself,
knew and loved us before time existed.
This Divine knowledge,
chose with the foreknowledge
of the Second Person of the Trinity,
who is love, to become our Mother.
This was our Father's intention;
our Mother brought it about;
and our Protector the Spirit
made it firm and real.
In God, we have our being.

We thank and praise our Father

for our creation;

we pray with our entire consciousness

to our Mother

for mercy and understanding;

and we ask our Protector

the Spirit

for help and grace.

The High God,

Sovereign Wisdom,

put on flesh

and mothered us in all things.

~~~~~~~~

Through the Divine Mother,

grace is spread out wide and long,

deep and high,

like a blanket

with no edges or binding.

Jesus is our True Mother.
All the qualities of motherhood
come from the Second Person of the Trinity,
where we are kept whole and safe,
both in our human nature
and by spiritual grace,
fed by Christ's particular sweetness.

In Mother Christ we are nurtured

so that we grow,

and in Mother Christ's mercy

we are reshaped, restored,

reunited with our spiritual essence,

through the power of Christ's endurance,

death, and resurrection.

This is our Mother's work

in all of us.

God's Motherhood

wears three faces:

first, the Divine Mother gave birth to us

and gave us life;

second, She shared our human lives;

and third, She works always to keep us safe.

And all is one love.

The Motherhood of mercy and grace

restores us to our true natures,

that which we were made to be

by the Motherhood of love,

the Motherhood of Being.

No one else could mother us

the way Christ does.

Our human mothers

bore us into a world of pain and death,

but our True Mother,

Jesus—All-Love—bears us

into joy and endless life.

(Blessed may She be!)

In this way, Mother Christ

supports and holds us

in love within Herself

(as a pregnant mother

holds her unborn child).

Yes, God is our Father,

and yes, God is also our Mother.

The Divine demonstrates this

in all that exists.

Motherhood is God.

~~~~~~~~

God is as much in the physical process

of birth's labor and delivery

as God is in the process

of our spiritual birth.

The Divine One says,

"I am the strength and goodness of Fatherhood;

I am the wisdom of Motherhood;

I am the Light and Grace

that comes from all true love;

I am the Trinity; I am Unity;

I am the authority of goodness

living in all things.

I am the One who makes you love;

I am the One who makes you yearn for more;

and I am the endless fulfillment

of all true desires."

Out of love,

God made human beings,

and that same love

became a human being.

~~~~~~~~~

Humanity's longings and desires

were made visible in Jesus.

We are the Humanity of Christ.
Christ is the Head of this Body
of which we are all members.

～～～～～

But Christ's Body,
in which all of us are knit together,
is not yet complete in its light and life,
and so Christ longs and thirsts,
just as when He hung from the Cross,
and He will continue to thirst
until the last human being
has entered into His joy.

Jesus is All-Humanity,

who shall be kept forever,

and All-Humanity

(the part of us that is kept always safe)

is Jesus: the Love of God,

all that humanity possesses

of humility, strength,

goodness, and patience.

The Divine Essence

is united with our own.

Within this unity,

God is the perfect human being,

for Christ knots to Himself

each and every individual

and thus becomes the Complete Human,

the essence of all humanity.

The face of Jesus

is always turned toward you,

and He longs for your face to look back at Him.

~~~~~~~~

When you do,

He draws out your inner face

so that it joins with your outer face,

unified with God and with each other,

in the true and eternal joy

that is Jesus.

All shall be well,

and all shall be well,

and absolutely everything shall be well.

~~~~~~

Just as the joyful Trinity

made everything out of nothing,

so the same Trinity will make well

all that is not well.

The Divine One not only pays attention

to high and great things,

things that are obvious and important,

but also, equally, to small things

that seem trivial, simple, and overlooked.

~~~~~~~~

This is what Jesus meant when He said,

"Absolutely everything shall be well."

Not even the least thing

will be forgotten.

What seems ugly and broken

is only temporary.

Ultimately, it is an illusion.

~~~~~~~~

All that was once bent and broken

will be made whole and straight,

by the sweet energy

of God.

Straight lines cannot be made straighter,

and God is the essence of straightness.

Each Divine action

is yet another line drawn true.

And just as God desires what is best

for each detail of Creation,

so does the Spirit lead all things

straight

to that goal.

~~~~~~~

All that God accomplishes increases Divine joy.

God makes God happy!

Make a space in your life

for looking at the Divine One,

and you will experience

all manner of comfort

and joy.

11

THE SOUL

Your spiritual essence

can rightly be called your soul—

but at the same time, your sense-based being

is also your soul.

This is because of the unity

of spirit and senses in God.

You may see them as two separate things,

but they are not.

~~~~~~~

Your truest essence is in God.

You are enclosed in the Divine,

and the Divine is enclosed in you.

Our souls are made one with God,

and so nothing exists

between God and our souls,

not anger, not even forgiveness,

for we are so completely united

with God's Unity

that nothing separates us

from the Divine Essence.

~~~~~~~~

We will be kept true to our real selves

and to God,

forever and ever.

The soul is large, an endless world,

a kingdom of delight,

a city of great worth.

In the center of the city

sits our Protector Jesus,

both God and Human,

highest Watcher over the realm,

most joyous and solemn King,

worthiest Protector,

clad in glory.

The Trinity

takes endless joy

in the human soul.

~~~~~~~

The Divine One knows

that which best suits God,

and the human soul suits God

endlessly and without beginning.

The Divine One gives our souls

great riches, excellence, and abilities,

and knots them to our bodies.

These soul-to-body knots

are what make us sense-creatures—

beings who perceive reality through our senses.

Our Protector Jesus

sits in the homestead of our sense-soul,

where He is enclosed,

and at the same time our own essence

is enclosed in Jesus,

while His Soul sits at rest

within the Divine Essence.

If we want to understand our own selves,

we must spend time communing with our souls,

enjoying them as a lover enjoys her beloved.

It makes sense then

that we also seek the Divine Protector,

in Whom our souls are enclosed.

We can never clearly know our own souls

until we know God.

In fact,

we can come to know God more easily

than we can know our own souls.

For our souls are rooted so deeply in God,

where they are endlessly treasured,

that we cannot truly know them

until we first know God,

the Soul-Maker,

with Whom our souls are united.

The human soul was made from nothing;
brought into being from nothing
that had previously been created.
When God made the human body, however,
the Divine Hand used the Earth's clay,
solid matter that is a mixture
of all the tiny pieces that make our world.
So you are both Nature-made,
and at the same time, you are not-made.
And what is the only thing that is not-made?
God!
That is why God truly lives in the human soul—
nothing between the Divine Essence and yours.

In your truest essence you are complete,

even if your sense-soul fails.

No part of your nature shall die,

for your highest aspects are tied to God

from the time they were made,

and meanwhile God is fastened

to the lower aspects of your nature

from the moment when your soul took flesh.

Through Christ,

the two aspects of your nature

are united and kept safe.

Your soul is knit to God
at the deepest level of your being,
with a knot so delicate and strong
that your soul is one with God,
made endlessly whole and clean and safe.
All souls everywhere
are eternally rescued by this same knot,
made one in this unity,
made whole and healthy
through Divine health.

Your soul was created to be God's home;

and your soul's home is God.

The Divine One who is your Maker

lives in your soul,

and your soul lives in the Divine Essence,

the very substance from which

it was created.

~~~~~~~

I can see no difference then

between the Divine Essence and our own:

all is God, though only God is God,

and our essence is a Divine creation

that lives within God.

In each soul

is a God-like piece,

a volition that never said yes

to separation from God

and never will.

Just as there is a selfish, lower piece in each of us

that wills separation and disunity,

so there is also a higher piece

that wants only good.

You can experience two opposite feelings
at one and the same time
because your nature has two aspects:
the one your external ego
and the other your inner spirit.
The ego is mortal, experiencing pain and sorrow.
That is just the way things will always be
in this life.
But the inner spirit can be mistress of the ego.
Though the ego does not disappear,
the spirit need not pay much attention
to its complaints,
for your spirit is capable of directing your ego.

The Divine One says,

"I will smash your empty desires,

your unhealthy selfishness—

and after that, I will gather you together,

completely clean, completely whole,

made one with Me."

~~~~~~~

In the end, both your outer persona

and your inner Self

will be united in joy

by the grace and strength of Christ.

You have been redeemed in love,

set free from all that would make you less than

you are called to be.

But in the temporal life you live on Earth,

your sense-soul seldom knows

what your true Self is.

You judge yourself
by looking at your changeable sense-soul,
which seems like one thing this minute
and another thing the next,
depending on where you direct your attention.
The perceptions of your sense-soul
are a mixed bag,
because you focus on so many different things.

~~~~~~~~

When you truly see
both God and your true Self,
then you shall find rest and peace.

The essence of who you are,

the very substance of your identity,

is in God,

and God is in not only your inner spirit

but also your sense-soul —

that which some call the ego,

your outer consciousness.

~~~~~~

God has made a treasure of unity

between your soul and your body.

Your soul grows with your body,
and your body with your soul,
each lending support to the other,
until you are mature,
as your own nature dictates.
And then, as you continue to grow,
rooted in the soil of this world
and nourished with Divine Mercy,
the Spirit breathes into you
the gifts that lead you to endless life.

You—and all humankind—shall be restored

out of double death into life,

through the Second Person of the Trinity,

who restores both your inner Self

and your outer sense-soul.

Jesus put on the physical substance

of human nature,

which is based on the perceptions

of our five senses,

while at the same time our highest essence

has always been one with God

from the moment of creation.

The Divine One
is nearer to you than your own soul,
for God is the soil in which your soul is rooted;
and Jesus is the Midpoint that unites
your eternal substance and your sense-soul,
so they can never be separated.

~~~~~~

Your soul sits at rest in God;
your soul stands up straight in God's strength;
and your soul's very nature
is rooted in God's endless love.

The Divine touch on your soul

is not something out of the ordinary.

It is grounded in the very nature

of your being.

~~~~~~~

The light that shines

from the City of the Self

is the splendor of your Protector's love.

At the exact point where your soul

is connected to your flesh and senses,

at that same point,

God built the Divine City,

the Divine Home,

a resting spot God never leaves.

God never departs from our souls;

the Divine Essence lives there with eternal joy.

God finds in you

the most comfortable home,

an endless dwelling place.

God delights

to make the Divine Kingdom within your mind;

to repose at rest within your soul;

and to dwell there endlessly,

so that you function within God,

your actions making you God's helper.

as you pay attention to God,

desiring that all your actions be God's actions,

placing your confidence in God.

In God's endless love,

your soul is kept whole.

In this endless love

you are led, kept safe;

you will never be lost,

for your safety is inherent

in the moment and method of your creation.

Your soul is alive,

filled with life that shall endure without end,

thanks to Divine sweetness and grace.

Your soul is driven forward by emotional cycles:

sometimes you are contented,

and sometimes you feel abandoned.

But your emotions are sensations,

without substance.

The Divine One keeps you equally safe

in sadness and in happiness.

Both sorrow and elation are gifts to you

from God.

God allows you to feel a range of emotions—

but they are all expressions of Divine love.

Despite your up-and-down feelings
of sadness and happiness,
the Divine One wants you to understand
and hold tight to the belief
that your being exists more in Heaven
than it does on Earth
When you experience depression and anxiety,
these sensations, like any temporary pain,
are to be endured until they pass—
and then you can return
to the endless enjoyment God offers you.

The sort of fear that makes you cling to God,

full of trust and confidence,

is the only type of fear that is good and true,

springing from Grace.

Fear that does not possess these qualities

is a crooked sort of thing

that pulls you out of alignment.

Be cautious of any fear

that makes you feel separated from the Divine.

Refuse to allow anything

that distorts the truth

to take root in your mind.

From your perspective,

you do nothing but seek and suffer.

You will not see with clarity

that you have found God

until Grace reveals this to you.

It is the seeking, with faith, hope, and love,

that pleases your Protector,

while it is the finding

that pleases you and fills you with joy.

And yet

longing is the road you travel,

and desire is your road map.

The Divine One never leaves you,
but during your earthly life,
seeking God is as useful to your soul
as seeing God.
Leave your awareness of the Divine Presence
up to God, in humility and trust,
to reveal to you as God wants.
Your only job is to cling to God,
regardless of your passing sensations.
Whether you see God or only seek to see God,
you add to the Divine Essence when you simply
fasten your mind and life there—

in God.

Seeking-and-asking
is a true, joyful, and enduring soul-quality,
a part of who you are as a human being.

~~~~~~

Even though God clasps you close
and is nearer to you
than tongue can tell or mind can think,
yet your yearning and sorrow will never end
until at last you clearly see the Divine Face
in all its friendliness and joy.
Then you will know that all is whole,
each good thing in your life
solid and unshaken.

In our ignorance and incomprehension of Love,

humans use many methods for asking God

for what they want.

But God is best worshipped —

and most delighted —

when we simply turn to the Divine One,

trusting totally in that Unity.

This reveals a deeper understanding of God

and creates in us an unshakeable love,

far more than any method of prayer

human minds could contrive.

Resting in Divine Unity is the highest prayer,

and it reaches down to your deepest needs.

It brings your soul to life;

it brings you more of life's fullness;

and your life expands with grace and strength.

This attitude of prayer

aligns most easily with your nature,

and it requires the least effort to achieve,

for it is simply what your soul already craves,

and what it shall always crave

until you truly understand

that you are wrapped in Divine Unity:

the goodness of God.

The Divine One says,
"I am the Ground of each thing
for which your soul yearns.
It is My will first that you have whatever it is,
and then I make you long for it,
and then you ask Me for it—
so why would I not then give you
that for which I have made you yearn?"
You do not make God act with your prayers,
as though you could move the Divine Essence
to be what you want,
but rather instead, the Divine One
already lives in your heart's desires.

The Divine One says,

"Pray inside your mind,

even if you feel no emotional satisfaction,

for it is good for you,

even if you can't feel the benefits,

even if you can't see them,

even if you think you are incapable of prayer.

In the midst of dryness and barrenness,

in your sadness and weakness,

your prayers always make Me happy,

even if you feel your prayer is flavorless and dry.

I treasure all your prayers."

Jesus, your Protector,

laughs with gladness

whenever He hears you praying.

He tends your prayers

and works through them to change your life.

~~~~~~~

Divine Grace makes you become like God,

not only because your soul is tied to Christ

with the bonds of family love and relationship,

but because you are becoming

more and more

like Him.

If you do not trust as much as you pray,
your prayers are empty
and you make your own life more difficult.
You don't really comprehend
that your Protector is the Ground
from which your prayers spring,
nor that your desires are given to you
by the generosity of Divine love.
If you grasped the reality of this,
you would have total confidence
that God will grant the desire's of your heart.

Prayer is like an arrow

shot straight toward joy's fulfillment

in Heaven—

and prayer is also like a shelter

that covers you with the knowledge

that you can trust God

to grant all for which you yearn.

~~~~~~~~

No one sincerely asks for Grace and Mercy

without having already been given

Grace and Mercy.

If you pray and see no answer,
you become weighed down with doubt,
and that profits no one.
But on the other hand, if you just sit back
and wait to see what God is doing
and never bother to unite yourself
with the Divine Verb through prayer,
then you are missing out,
not investing in the work God is doing,
and you diminish its action
in your own soul.

There are many times
when we cannot perceive the Divine Presence
and then we go to Jesus, hungry and needy,
reliant on prayer to enable us to go on.
For when storms toss your soul,
when you feel lonely and troubled,
then you need to pray,
so you will become pliable in God's Hand,
supple and responsive to the Divine Will.
(Remember, though,
prayer does not shape the Divine Will
so that it flows in one direction or another,
for God is always the same in love.)

Your soul is like God in its essence,

and it is woven into the Divine One

with bonds of kinship—

yet your way of life often separates you from God.

Prayer is an affirmation

that realigns your soul with the Divine Will.

Prayer is a conduit for Grace,

for God wants to make you a partner

in all the good the Divine Will accomplishes.

Prayer matches your mind

to God's.

When the Divine One is revealed,

your prayers are struck dumb.

This is a mountaintop prayer, a prayer that lies

beyond your senses and human faculties.

In this moment, the strands of all your prayers

are pulled together into a single cord

and then a single point—

God.

And there they remain . . .

until the Divine Will once more stirs you

to remember all your other prayers,

the details of your life.

Simply enjoying your soul's Protector

is the best prayer.

~~~~~~~~

Giving thanks is a part of prayer,

a true heart-knowledge.

Your mind and soul
are often restless and uncomfortable,
because you rely on things that are so small,
which can offer you no real rest or security.
When you willingly, lovingly detach your mind
from the world around you,
you will find the One who is all—
and your soul will be at rest.
No soul finds peace
until it achieves nothingness
even in the midst of the created world.

Do not allow yourself

to become too attached

to individual aspects of Creation,

but instead, enjoy the Divine worth in everything.

This means you will not be greatly distressed

if you lose one aspect of your life,

for you can rest in the confidence

that the whole of reality is still fine—

for absolutely everything shall be well.

Look at the big picture

rather than the small.

See Divine Grace in everything around you.

It is worth more to your soul

if you can perceive the Divine Presence in all life

rather than merely in one specific creation.

~~~~~~~~

The Divine One is pleased when you rest

in the Spirit's presence,

since all that was created will never be enough

in and of itself

to give you what you need.

Faith is a strength

that the Spirit brings

out from your nature-substance

into your sense-soul,

and through this, all other strengths come.

Without faith, you are weak,

for faith is merely a straight and direct

understanding

(a true belief, a deeply rooted trust)

in who you are—

that you are in God,

and God is in you.

Only when you reach the glad and friendly

Presence of the Divine

will you climb again as high

as you did in childhood.

When you were a child,

your strength and intelligence

were not fully developed yet,

and yet your soul will never climb as high,

not in this life.

as it did in childhood.

Only children

have the strength to fully believe.

III

SIN AND SORROW

Sin is exile and separation from God.

~~~~~~~

All action is God,

and sin is no action at all.

~~~~~~~

God is all reality,

and sin is the absence of reality.

Sin has no substance, no being.

In effect, it does not exist,

for it can only be known through the pain

it causes.

Pain purifies you,

teaches you about yourself,

and that makes you rely on Divine kindness.

~~~~~~

Because your Protector loves you so tenderly,

the Divine One is quick to comfort, saying,

"Granted, sin has caused you all this pain,

but all shall be well, and all shall be well,

and absolutely everything shall be well."

These words are said with so much love,

with no hint of blame.

If God does not blame me for sin,
I would be rude to blame God for it!
The Divine One and I are family,
connected by intimate bonds,
and guilt and blame have no part
in such a relationship.

Do not focus on sin,

either your own or another's.

Instead, seek Divine healing and strength

on behalf of us all,

and when you look at another

who has fallen into sin,

focus only on compassion

and your own brokenness,

longing for God's healing for you both.

Without this attitude, your soul

will trip and stumble into sin.

Compassion is your protection.

Thinking about sin,

whether your own or another's,

creates a spiritual fog

that robs from you

the sight of God's beauty.

Sin—separating yourself from God—

is the most pain you will ever experience.

Sin is like a knife that scrapes off your skin,

a whip that beats you to the point

that you look hateful to yourself,

so that you think you are good for nothing

but to be buried in hell.

And there you sink,

until your bruises are transformed

into the Spirit's touch on your soul,

and then sin's bite serves to send you leaping

forward into God's mercy.

Whenever your thoughts
turn to self-condemnation,
your Protector God touches you gently,
getting your attention,
calling you with joy, speaking to your soul:
"Let love fill you, My dear child.
Turn to Me—I am enough for you—
and take joy in your Rescuer
and in your safety and wholeness."
Even if you did nothing but sin,
your sin could do nothing
to stop the action of Divine sweetness.

With deep tenderness,

your Protector keeps you,

even when it seems to you that you are forsaken,

as though you have been

thrown out in the garbage because of your sin,

just as you feel you deserve.

But your bruises give you compassion for others

and a sincere longing for God.

When you reach that point,

you are suddenly delivered from your pain,

taken up into Heaven,

and transformed into a saint.

The Divine One

views sin as a lover looks

at a beloved's sorrow and pain;

God puts no mark of blame on those who sin.

The consequence of sin is not insignificant,

and yet it can bring light and life and healing.

And so shall shame be transformed

into greater worth and deeper joy.

~~~~~~~~

Your Protector does not want you to despair

no matter how often or how badly you fall,

for your failures cannot hinder

Divine love.

JULIAN OF NORWICH

There is no deeper hell than sin.
In fact, there is no hell at all except for sin.

Sin separates your sense-soul
from its perception of the Divine Presence.
When your perceptions are no longer clouded,
then God welcomes you
with laughter and a glad face,
as if you had just come home
after a painful prison sentence,
The Divine One says,
"My darling, I'm so glad you can see Me again!
Now you know we are always together."

In this life, we live in a storm of sorrow and pain,

simply because we are blind:

We cannot see God.

If we could see God,

continually and clearly,

then we would have no impulse

to separate ourselves from the Divine Presence;

none of our actions and desires

would lead to sin.

Our sin turns us into outcasts

from peace and love.

But God's face is always turned toward us,

waiting.

We often lose sight of God.
We become preoccupied with selfish concerns,
and everything seems wrong.
Our lives no longer align with Divine joy;
we feel as though we are at opposite poles
from God.
This disjointedness from the Divine Will
is the meaning of original sin.
This is what causes our pain and storms;
this is what makes us feel separated from God;
and this is what causes all
spiritual and physical suffering.

Mercy pays the price for our sin—

it reverses what would have been

the natural consequences of our blindness.

Mercy is sweet and generous,

a work of love that mingles

with abundant compassion.

Mercy acts to keeps us safe,

and Mercy works to transform

all that touches us

into good.

You have within you
a marvelous mingling of health and wounds,
wholeness and sorrow,
for you contain in your being
both Jesus your Risen Protector
and Adam, who fell into death.
In Christ, you are kept steadfastly safe—
but at the same time, you are terribly broken,
your emotions and vision shattered
by Adam's fall,
so that you experience pain,
separation, and darkness.

When you sin,
neither wallow in despair
nor become reckless,
treating sin as though it didn't matter;
instead, honestly acknowledge your weakness
as you stand naked before God,
accepting that in your own strength
you cannot keep your balance
for even the blink of an eye.
All you can do is cling to God.

~~~~~~~~

Christ your Protector
guards your inmost being.

God's viewpoint
is totally different from yours.
Your role is to search out your sins
and weaknesses,
examining yourself with deep humility—
but meanwhile, the role of your Protector God
is to look past all your weakness,
calling you always upward
into Divine sweetness and unity.
The outward reality
has the appearance of weakness,
while the inner reality
is that of endless love.

Divine Mercy

went with the All-Human into Hell,

and kept us safe there.

~~~~~~~

Once you are united with the High Self,

what you thought were failures

will be turned into an endless treasure.

Within your soul there lives a will
that never agreed to be separated
from the Divine, nor ever will agree,
despite the appearance
of external circumstances.
This aspect of your soul is the Divine Will
living in you, which can never say yes to evil;
instead, it always leans toward goodness,
and it works for the unity of all things.
A piece of your very essence
remains always whole and safe
in Jesus Christ, your Divine Protector.

In Eternity,

all created beings will be knit tight to God,

fulfilled by the Divine alignment and unity—

but this will only be possible because all along

a part of Creation's deepest substance

was never separated from God,

nor ever could be

because of the Divine Vision,

endless and unlimited,

that works with the Divine Will,

drawing straight lines toward the single Point

where all is One.

When you take your leave
of Christ's mind within you,
when you neglect to keep your soul whole—
then Christ keeps you whole by Himself,
standing guard over you
with sorrow and yearning.
When you put yourself outside of Him
because of your despair, or laziness,
then you leave your Protector
standing all alone
within your soul.

You are like a dead person,

unable to see the reality of your own joyous life.

And yet you are not dead in God's sight

nor does the Divine Presence ever leave you.

You feel as though you are in mortal danger,

as though you were in a region of hell,

but it is only the sorrow and pain

within your own mind that you feel.

The Divine does not want you

exiled from yourself.

Instead, God wants you to turn back

to the Divine Presence within you,

for you are God's delight.

What is it in this life

that separates you into two pieces?

Is it evil?

Or is it good?

In that it serves to help you grow, it is good

(for it heals you and unites you with God)—

but in that it makes you lose your sense

of who you are in the Divine,

then it is evil.

God guides you to hold tight to the Divine,

to fasten yourself to God

in the most intimate way possible,

forever,

in whatever condition you find yourself,

whether you are clean or dirty in your own eyes,

for God's love for you never changes.

~~~~~~~

Whether you are well or ill,

whole or broken,

Christ wants you

to never run away from Him.

You need to see your sin clearly,
so that you lose your false pride
and presumption, so that you understand
how you have become bent
from the shape God wanted for you.
As your Protector shows you
the smallest glimpses of your true reality,
you will be able to throw yourself forward
toward the full reality
you cannot see.

The more needy you are,

the more you need

to touch the hem of the Divine Presence.

When you become aware

that you are broken and exiled,

you flee to your Protector—and in your flight,

you are healed.

~~~~~~~~~

Divine love

is endless

and unchangeable

Oh Exiled One,

separated from God

and from your own sense of yourself!

What are you?

You are nothing.

When I saw that God had made all things,

I saw no sinners such as you.

And when I saw my Protector Jesus

in my soul—sharing His worth with me,

His love, His pleasure, His authority,

and all that He has made—I did not see you.

And that is why I am certain

that you are truly nothing.

Anything that has to do with your false self

is nothing,

and it shall be endlessly and totally overthrown.

May God shield you

from all that separates you

from yourself

and from God.

Let it be so in love.

God allows troubles to enter our lives.

In the Divine Eye, these have no shame,

even though others may regard them with scorn.

When you are abused and violated,

snatched out of your sense of who you are,

you are at the same time

rescued from this life's emptiness,

and your path toward Heaven

is clear.

Your trials are not punishments.

Your failures

and your confusion

are both contained

within the Mercy of God.

Your Protector wants you
to help yourself with a wide-open mouth
to as much as you can
of the comfort and direction God offers you,
focusing all your attention there—
while at the same time, you only nibble
at this world's troubles and discomfort,
setting them aside as insignificant.
The less you focus on them,
the less important they will feel,
and the less they will bother you.

Even in those times
when you are in so much pain and distress
that you cannot focus on anything
but your feelings,
you can rest assured that these sensations
count for nothing; you can pass over them lightly,
without paying much attention to them.
As you come to know God better,
you shall have peace.
Everything God does will create in your mind
an enclosed garden of joy and delight,
a place where you can be safe
and happy.

Christ did not say,

"You'll never encounter storms,

you'll never have troubles,

you'll never be afflicted."

What He said was,

"You shall not be overcome."

One day,

you shall be taken from all your pain,

sickness, despair, and distress,

and you shall be filled with love and delight.

Then nothing will distress you;

no sluggishness will weaken you.

Joy and light will be yours endlessly.

Knowing this waits for you,

why should you be so upset

about this world's temporary discomforts?

On the day you die,

you shall come higher,

into God's Realm.

~~~~~~~~

Your life will be

forever fulfilled

at last.

When God rescues you from this life,

not only will you receive the same friendly joy

that other souls have experienced in Eternity,

but you will also receive a new, unique delight

all your own,

which will flow without limit from God,

filling you full.

This is the heavenly merchandise

God always planned to give you,

the treasure God keeps hidden for you,

waiting until the time

when you have grown enough

to be able to receive it.

When the Last Day comes,

and we are all brought up from this world,

then we shall see in God all the secrets

that are now hidden.

And not one of us will want to say,

"But if only . . ."

Instead, with one voice we shall say,

"Be blessed, Protector God,

for all is as it is,

and all is completely good."

The grace of the Spirit calls to you,

all through your life and even as you die,

filling you always with the longing to be loved.

And then, as you leave this life,

you will enter your Protector,

and you will clearly know at last.

You will fully have God,

and God will have you, endlessly and totally.

You will truly see God, fully feel God,

clearly hear God.

You will drink God; you will swallow God.

How sweet

is the taste of the Divine!

Our entire life,

all the weakness and dullness

we experience here,

is actually only a single point

from which we shall step suddenly

into such wide and endless delight

that all our pain

will disappear into nothingness.

God does not want us to dread

that which is unknown

but instead to rest in love and joy.

~~~~~~~

Our faith is a natural light,

an innate understanding,

that indicates the coming of endless day.

Light is carefully measured out to you,

so that you have what you need

to get through the night.

This light gives you life,

even while the night is dark

with pain and sadness.

God thanks you for enduring the darkness.

With Mercy and Grace, you can hold firm,

believing that the light is real,

and that you can follow it

with wisdom and strength.

The light is never so great

that you see complete daylight,

nor is it ever kept from you

so that utter darkness falls.

It is just enough light

for you to live as you need.

And when all sadness ends,

suddenly your eyes will open.

In the clear daylight,

your vision will be complete.

Your faith gives light to your night,

and that same light is God,

your endless Day.

IV

THE MEANING OF JULIAN'S VISION

Do you want to clearly see

the Protector's meaning in these showings?

Well, then, learn it well:

Love was God's meaning.

Who showed me these visions?

Love.

What was I shown?

Love.

Why was I shown these visions?

For love.

Hold on to love,

and you will learn and understand

more about Divine love—

but you will never learn

nor understand

anything else

about the God.

~~~~~~~

In love, you see God endlessly,

world without end.

This book is begun by God's gift,

by Divine grace,

but I do not believe it has yet been finished.

It is still developing and growing.

~~~~~~~~

Take it

from my heart to yours,

and then carry it out

into the world.

If you forget everything else,

remember this:

love is everything.

Love is God.

ALL SHALL BE WELL

A Modern-Language Version
of the Revelation of JULIAN OF NORWICH

by ELLYN SANNA

Paperback Price: $24.95

E-book Price: $8.99

"One of the 25 books every Christian should read."
—**Renovaré**

The great spiritual classic by Julian of Norwich is now available in modern, easy-to-comprehend language that stays true to Julian's original meanings. Her ancient wisdom is as relevant now as it was in the 14th century's world of plague, prejudice, and war. Discover Julian's joyous affirmation of the certainty of Divine love, a love that overcomes all.

THE HEART OF MEDITATION
INTERFLOW:
THOUGHTS, PRAYERS, & MEDITATIONS

by GEORGE BREED

Paperback Price: $14.95

In this paperback collection of the e-book series titled *Meditations of the Heart*, the author offers bite-size entries into mindfulness and transformation. Each meditation could be used as a vehicle for greater consciousness—or as a prayer leading to deeper awareness of spiritual reality and being. One Amazon reviewer summarized: "Each tiny gem of a meditation holds meaning beyond and beneath the words, and each provides nourishment for the mind and the heart. Concise, simple, but packed with a powerful load of thought-provoking enlightenment, George Breed gives more to us in his meditations with a dozen or so words than most philosophers give in twelve dozen."

CELTIC NATURE PRAYERS
Prayers from an Ancient Well

by KENNETH MCINTOSH with LUCIE STONE

Paperback Price: $14.95

E-book Price: $5.99

Find God in Nature

Pray for Our Endangered Planet

Commune with God in nature using these ancient and modern prayers, compiled and written by Kenneth McIntosh, author of the bestselling *Water from an Ancient Well: Celtic Spirituality for Modern Life.* Just as the Celts found the Divine in every tree and blade of grass, so we too can be refreshed and enriched by a new connection with the Earth.

Love Prayers
from Rumi & other Sufi Mystics

edited by DEVON HOLCOMBE

Paperback Price: $16.95

The Sufi mystics' religion was love–and God was their Beloved. Their relationship with the Beloved gave each moment meaning and joy.

As you pray with words inspired by Rumi and other Sufi mystics, you'll experience a new understanding of the Divine One who is everything and nothing, all that we can perceive and all that we cannot. You may even, like the Sufis, find yourself falling head over heels in love with a God who is present everywhere, within you and without. Whatever your religion (or lack of religion), these spiritual poems, inspired by ancient Sufism, will bring you into a deeper relationship with both the Divine and your true Self.

www.AnamcharaBooks.com

www.ingramcontent.com/pod-product-compliance
Lightning Source LLC
Chambersburg PA
CBHW060525080526
44586CB00012B/622